POSITIVE VIBES ~3~

"FIRESIDE THOUGHTS"

PRESTON MITCHUM JR.

Positive Vibes 3, Fireside Thoughts

ISBN: 978-1-956581-26-3

Canyon Lake, Texas
www.ErinGoBraghPublishing.com

INTRODUCTION

No matter what is going on around author Preston Mitchum, Jr., he is always looking for that positive perspective on the situation. He celebrates the good times and looks for ways to learn through the tough ones. In this third book, his message remains:

Positive Thoughts, Positive Vibes.

Having received such incredible feedback from his ever-increasing number of readers and social media followers, Preston put pen to paper once again to bring you even more positivity in our ever-changing and sometimes tumultuous world.

Whether you read these messages back-to-back, or every once in a while, the goal is to help boost your perception of life, take time to appreciate it and find the positives that are all around us.

God has given us such an amazing gift - this life.

Let's show our appreciation for it by cherishing each and every moment.

TABLE OF CONTENTS

Many of you know, by now, that I love spending time by the fire. My mind is drawn into the flames which provides a sense of peacefulness. The flames, stars and cool summer breeze can provide the perfect relaxing evening. Many of the affirmations written in this book called "Fireside Thoughts" came while taking in the warmth of the burning flames. When the soul is soothed, magical things can happen. Creating a space to be free of distraction and allowing the juices to flow.

The intimacy and connection of the encounters from the many relationships we have had, shape us into the humans we are today. I enjoy soaking in the many conversations and insight gathered along my journey. I hope that this book, along with my others, will open your eyes and awaken your soul.

Fireside Thoughts

Fireside Thoughts

You know what I did last night? I sat back, outside by my chimenea and gazed into the fire. That's right, allowing the sun to set and the moon to shine.

Sitting by a nice fire and gazing upwards at the starry night gave me an opportunity to be at one with myself. It gave me an opportunity to relax and be present.

Yes, being present is so important. There is something about the off-rhythm crackle of the flames, just by watching them, focuses your mind. What do you see? What do you feel when you stare into the fire? Is it a moment of peace to clear your mind and rebalance your soul? Let the fireside warm your spirit.

Relax by the Fire

There is nothing like relaxing next to a nice fire. Grab some twigs or logs, start up the fire pit and then gaze into the stars. When you sit back and stare into the fire, you get away for a little while. Another opportunity has presented itself to breathe. Yes, summer nights can be muggy, but gaze onto the stars and allow your mind to relax. We all have different ways to relax, understanding what works for you is key. What gives you that moment to see and feel good? Life's problems, and the hustle and bustle of the world will be there when you get back.

GET COMFY

All right now don't you go laughing at me, I like to get comfy. Yes, that's what I call it, getting "Comfy." I can easily post myself up at a restaurant, grab a nice drink, and sit there for hours just relaxing. It's called being at peace with myself.

I call it getting comfy, you might call it something else. Either way, it's that opportunity for us to just 'be' and not allow any noise to distract us. It provides the opportunity to rebalance ourselves. So, make sure you take some time today to get comfy.

POSITIVE THOUGHTS, POSITIVE VIBES!

The Need to Feel

Keith Whitley said it best, "Love me tonight, hold me tight, and don't close your eyes." Tonight, is the night I don't want to end.

The ability and need to 'feel' is running through me. I need you like oxygen, to breathe and keep taking breaths. I need this to fuel the positive energy that is needed. I needed to feel you mind, body and soul because what you give me feels like nothing I've ever felt before. Allowing me to be free and feel free in a space that is just right. Love me tonight in a way that will never end as we close our eyes to rest. In hopes to behold what tomorrow has to offer.

SILENCE

Sometimes saying nothing is the best thing. Your silence means that you are listening. Listening to every single word that I'm saying.

I can see it in your eyes that you're engaged in the words coming from my mouth, and through that, I know the space is safe.

Thank you for offering up a safe space and showing me with your eyes that love is present.

POSITIVE THOUGHTS, POSITIVE VIBES!

SEARCH FOR BALANCE

Are you in search for that something that makes your spirit feel good? It can come in all form's shapes, and sizes, through people, things, and of course what you are passionate about. It's very important to put yourself around positive energy and positive people. It feels like a fresh cool breeze or a fresh cup of orange juice.

Never stop searching for something that makes your spirit feel good, this is what helps create the balance in our lives. The ability to create balance is so important. So, continue to search for the things that make you feel good.

Be Present

Relationships are so important to our everyday well-being. Family, friends, lovers they all hold different energies to keep us balanced. Keeping the communication lines open with honesty will lead to understanding. Through understanding comes respect and with respect comes presence.

The ability to be who you are, in state of where you are, allows for the relationships to grow positively. It's all about the people and energy that surrounds you, which allows your spirit to feel free. Enjoy those wonderful relationships and accept them in whatever form they hold. Be present!

HAVE AN OPEN MIND

Every time I turn around, God continues to bless me. I pause and recognize all of the wonderful blessings that I have around me.

It's so important to take a step back and recognize all the wonderful things that you have; health, family, home, car and of course some peace. Moving forward, growing, learning and soaking in all the good the world has to offer.

Through this, the blessing will continue. Some might be big, and most will be very small. Some of us are always looking for the big things and we miss out on the little ones. Thank you, Lord, for giving me an open mind so I can accept and recognize the blessings.

PROVIDED PEACE

Its deep, real deep and you can't figure it out. You turn right you turn left. You call your best friend, neighbor you might even have a conversation with the dog, but you just can't figure it out. Something just doesn't feel right and you can't put a finger on it.

Allow God to provide the peace that you need, to minimize the noise, so you can figure out what is going on. There's an old saying, you have a friend in Jesus, and today might be the day you can call upon him to get you through.

POSITIVE THOUGHTS, POSITIVE VIBES!

Ecclesiastics 3:12-13

*I know that there is nothing better
for people than to be happy and to do
good while they live. That each of them
may eat and drink, and find satisfaction
in all their toil—
this is the gift of God.*

Take a Moment

Maybe now is the opportunity for you to take a step back and take care of you. Look within, take a moment to find tune yourself! Take a moment just to be at peace with yourself, love yourself and accept the beautiful person you are.

It's growth mode season and some doors are about to open for you. Clear out some of the old for some really good new. This will help attract the right person or persons to be in your space. People come into our lives at just the right time. Embrace the energy they give and allow that to enhance you on your journey.

THE GREAT OUTDOORS!

My youngest son, Harrison, loves being outside, whether he’s catching bugs or looking for slugs late at night, being outdoors makes him happy.

God's little creatures can offer a sense of gratification. Whether it’s riding scooters, or swinging on a swing, take a few minutes to enjoy the peacefulness of the outdoors. It's simplistic, no drama, no over thinking.

Nature allows you to just be and enjoy what life has to offer. You might be surprised how good it makes your spirit feel.

POSITIVE THOUGHTS, POSITIVE VIBES!

Being in the Moment

In Your Presence

Have I told you lately that I love being around you? The way you make me feel, make me laugh. I just enjoy being in your presence. Maybe it feels good having you in my life.

I love how we are able to sit and talk for hours. I love the positive energy that you exude that makes me feel so good. I can't wait to get together again so you can rejuvenate my mind, body and soul. Being in your presence makes me feel so good.

Today and every day, I wanna make sure you know; I just love the positive vibes you have brought into my life.

CREATE A FOUNDATION

I feel so blessed. I have the best kids, and the perfect neighbors in the perfect neighborhood. I'm grateful to have all of the basic things that sometimes, we take for granted. It's so important for us, every morning, to thank God for all that we have. Through my Foundation www.pmjfoundation.org I see the struggles many families are going through.

As we continue to move forward, take note that it all starts now, in the present. Create that solid foundation now that will create the balance you need in the future.

POSITIVE THOUGHTS, POSITIVE VIBES!

FIND THE TRUE 'YOU'

I thought I was living my best life… car, house, marriage you name it. I was moving too fast. I didn't take a step back to realize that I need to find myself. That's right, who the heck am I?

Make sure to take care of yourself, find out who you are so you don't lose yourself in the midst of trying to live your best life. It all starts from within, going deep down and letting the true 'you' come out. How cool is it, when you're able to find out who you are and what your purpose, passion and reason for living is? Yes, car, house and marriage can enhance your happiness but finding the true 'you' is priceless.

LAUGH

Look at you. Now, doesn't it feel good to be laughing again? I love seeing people laugh so hard, they hit the floor. You've been through some challenging times, but now you are feeling your best. You are living your best life and your laugh says it all.

POSITIVE THOUGHTS, POSITIVE VIBES!

DREAM

Dreamers, keep on dreaming! Who said that your dreams are not possible?

Yes, we don't know the future but if we stay in the now we can understand ourselves. Grab what you know and start with that. The road will get hard and you might not know where to turn. Just pick up the pieces and reclaim what is yours.

Most successful people have stumbled a few times. So, stand up tall and don't allow anything or anyone to knock you down.

You've got this!

POSITIVE THOUGHTS, POSITIVE VIBES!

YOUR EYES

They say it's all in the eyes! They reveal our mood, feelings and even emotions. Eyes can convey a warm, bright and inviting positive vibe that touches the soul. There is kindness in your eyes and you need to share it. It's like a warm subtle flame of goodness and trust. Through your eyes a glow appears that releases positive vibes, the ones that can heal, replenish and provide a safe space. The energy from the inside exude through your beautiful eyes, providing a sense of peace. Just for second the negativity of the world vanishes away.

I'VE CHANGED!

I was sitting here wondering why I don't look the same. I've changed! That's what it is, everything deep down inside feels a little different, my talk, walk and outlook on life. My smile is a little wider, my soul feels a little better and everyone says I'm wearing a glow. You know why? I took some time to focus on me. That's right, me!

Many of us spend so much time pleasing others that we forget about ourselves. Call it what you want, self-care, self-love… Create those boundaries and take care of 'you' for a change. Now you know why you don't look the same.

POSITIVE THOUGHTS, POSITIVE VIBES!

CHANGE COMES IN ALL FORMS

Just because it works for you doesn't mean it will work for someone else. We all have our own road and journey to travel. It's hard enough to make our own life changes so trying to help or guide others can be difficult.

Our changes come at the right time and we have to be in the right space to accept them. Someone else might not be there yet. So, when offering advice and suggestions to others, take that into consideration. Change comes in all forms and someone else's change might not be yours to handle.

BALANCE YOURSELF

I wasn't sure how I would get through it. I wasn't sure how I was going to get past it, and it took some time for me to break free. It was time for me to breathe again. It's so important that we continue to balance ourselves to make sure we're surrounded by people who will energize our mind, body, and soul.

I thought I had reached the end of the road until my angel appeared. That's right. If we keep our eyes open, that person will appear to lift our spirits and make themselves available.

That's in the Past

The world has a funny way of loving us sometimes. It doesn't always allow us to know our worth. Yes, I know you stumbled, tripped over, and can sometimes barely hold yourself up. That's in the past, and today you're going through your growth and cleansing process and understand that God has a bigger plan for you.

Your life is bigger than you, and once you start to understand your worth, you will understand your place along your journey. We all make mistakes. We all have done things that, maybe, we're not so proud of, or happy about, but all of that is in the past and today you're living in the present.

LOVE YOURSELF

Some of us struggle from loving on the inside and the outside of our bodies. We're wandering around trying to figure out where the love went and how do we love again. Some of that could come from past experiences being hurt, giving too much with very little in return. Breakup, divorce, abandonment can play a major part in how you view and interpret love.

Don't let the past hold you from what in the present. Take those experiences as life lessons and work on loving yourself all over again. You might have been broken in the past but keep picking up those pieces and forming that new you.

REST THE SPIRIT

Take care of your spirit to fuel your physical self. Your spiritual self is the most important component of your being. You must do things and surround yourself with people who energize your spirit. If your spirit feels good most times your body will follow.

Nutrition and exercise are very important as well. Balance yourself by getting your spirit in the right place. You need both your spiritual and physical self to be balanced so the world is getting the best of You!

POSITIVE THOUGHTS, POSITIVE VIBES!

REFLECTIONS

Take a look in the mirror; what do you see? Our personal experiences shape how we view ourselves. Do you like what you see? Are you happy with the person you are?

Today is the day you accept yourself, love who you are, and try to embrace the changes you need to make in your life.

Bit by bit, piece by piece, you will continue to shape the person in the mirror. Looking into the mirror gives you a chance to reflect within. Love who you are because we all have something positive to share.

POSITIVE THOUGHTS, POSITIVE VIBES!

YOUR HOME

They say home is where the heart is. My oldest son, Carter, will ask "Daddy, what are we doing today?" I answer, "Not sure, what would you like to do?" He replies, "Stay home."

There is a comfort in being in the space you call home. It is a place where you feel love, safe and at peace.

Many of us search all of our lives looking for a place we can call home. Sometimes, the space is right in front of you. The simplicity of it is what we should look for.

Home is where the heart is so let your heart be at home.

Romans 15:13

May the God of hope fill you
with all joy and peace
as you trust in him,
so that you may overflow
with hope by the power
of the Holy Spirit.

YOUR HAPPY PLACE

How cool is it that you have a happy place? Yes, we all need one. A place that provides peace in the midst of the storm. They call it 'Stormy Monday' as we all wait for Friday to come. That is not the way to live. We should love every day. Be able to enjoy the blessings of each day God gives us. Maybe you can transfer some of the awesome things about your happy place into day-to-day living. Peace can be found all around us if we just look for it. Push the negativity aside and allow happiness within yourself.

POSITIVE THOUGHTS, POSITIVE VIBES!

TAKE TIME FOR YOU

I hear you. You're not asking for much, maybe a nice dinner, little glass of wine, back rub. You've had a long day and those feet of yours are tired. Sometimes we're not surrounded by that special someone that can offer those things.

But it's important that you find a little time for self-care. Your mental and physical health allows you to take care of all the things needed. Put aside a few things today, take a moment to meditate, read a book, pour your own glass of wine or take a nice walk.

RESTING YOUR MIND

THE FIRST STEP

God is waiting for you to make the first step.

Fannie Lou Hamer said it best, "You can pray until you faint, but unless you get up and try to do something, God is not going to put it in your lap." Now that is the truth!

Today is the day of change, by making the first step he will put positive people in your pathway to help with the others. No need to hold back on the opportunity for positivity to take control. Your mind, body and soul are focused on seeing the change, and now it takes all of us working together to create it!

A GRATEFUL ATTITUDE

I'm sitting here laughing at my attitude. I've allowed the world to pour all of its negativity on me, and my attitude is in the dumps. The best part about this whole situation is that I've recognized it, so it's up to me to create the change. Start with gratitude and being grateful for all of the things that I have in my life. I might just take a moment to meditate. Go for a walk, clear my mind so that I can change the attitude from within. No matter what the world throws at us, we always have to remember we have control of ourselves. Sometimes changing the circumstances, situations, or just walking away for a second, can be the deciding factor in changing your attitude in a positive direction.

Break Through the Noise

I’ve got joy deep down in my soul. What could give you joy that feels that good? In most cases, it is something simple! A sunset, a walk by the lake, a smile or hug from that special someone.

It’s usually the little things in life that bring us joy. Today you might be having a hard time finding or feeling that joy. It's there; you just got caught up in the noise. Break through the noise, turn down the volume, and get back to the joy. Take a moment to feel from within.

Never allow the noise to steal your joy!

FIND THE BALANCE

Man, I just keep on giving, giving and giving but not sure what I'm getting in return. Being a giving person, that's what I know how to do, GIVE! I hear ya, you've given so much that you are kind of burnt out. Today might be the day to just take a step back for a moment and take some time out for you. It's not selfish to think about the well-being of you. You don't really need anything in return. What you need is balance. I've said it often, surrounding yourself with people who raise and lift you up. Sometimes the return is just making sure you take the time out to rebalance, reorganize and rejuvenate yourself. Giving is important, but we also have to make sure that we don't burn ourselves out. They call it creating boundaries. Create some boundaries for yourself that will make sure you provide the balance that you need.

YOU ARE IMPORTANT!

Always remember the importance of you!

Every one of us plays an important role in creating history. Our lives will not only be shaped by our experiences, but the choices we make. The life you live continues to impact the ones around even if you don't recognize it.

Someone is watching, listening and taking in your light. Allow it to shine and never underestimate your possibilities of making a positive impact.

Walk, talk and live with a purpose for the importance of you is valuable to the world.

POSITIVE THOUGHTS, POSITIVE VIBES!

THE HEALING PROCESS

How do we go through the healing process? When is it time to recognize that there are things within you that need healing in order to move forward? What does the healing process look like? Is this something that you can do alone, or is this something that takes help from others? The first step is, recognizing that you're hurt or something is damaged within that needs healing. You really can't put a timetable on how long it will take for you to go through this process but recognizing it is the biggest thing. You will travel on your journey with stumbling blocks, pitfalls and detours. When the time is right for you, the healing process will take place.

SMELL THE ROSES

There's a saying, "Take some time to smell the roses." It means, take a moment and enjoy the beauty that is all around you.

This is a great way to start creating positivity in your life. Take a moment to enjoy the flowers, birds, the sunset, and a full moon. Don't run around all day and ignore what is simply beautiful around you.

Beauty represents good, and the good was created by God. Open your eyes to His creations and enjoy your ability to take it in.

POSITIVE THOUGHTS, POSITIVE VIBES.

A CHILD'S LOVE

And a child shall lead them. One of the greatest gifts God gives us is children. Pure and innocent, they come into the world just needing love and guidance.

This is also one of the greatest responsibilities as well. As parents, you give your all and in return they give you unconditional love. Love for our children comes in all different forms and wanting the best for them is universal.

Allow their purity and innocence to help lead your steps. You will be surprised how much you will learn.

POSITIVE THOUGHTS, POSITIVE VIBES!

IN THEIR PRESENCE

You know exactly what I'm talking about. That someone, your person or persons, that just makes you feel good. Being in their presence is what you've been urging for.

When you think of them, they make you smile, laugh, and provide a little bit of peace when needed. It's like pure joy being in their presence.

Minutes, hours, or even a few months can go by and the feeling never changes. They offer a safe space for you to "just be". Allowing your heart to be open and your soul to be filled. Hold on to the ones that fill your mind, body and soul with the peace you deserve.

THE POWER OF INTIMACY

The connection between two people can add positivity to one's life. One can define intimacy as, any action that enhances the mind/heart connection between two people. Even just sitting quietly holding hands is intimate with the right person.

Connection is important. It allows the mind, body and soul to grow and evolve. Be willing to feel the intimacy one has to offer and enjoy the beauty it holds.

RECONNECT

If we've learned anything, we know that people need people! It's time to go out there and get your groove back, offer up a hug, smile, a kind word. During these past few years, we all needed each other to get through some tough times. Now we could all use some cheering….

The power of physical connection is so important to the mind, body and soul. Yes, we figured it out, how to get by without it, but it sure feels good to get back to those old times of connection.

POSITIVE THOUGHTS, POSITIVE VIBES!

Deuteronomy 33: 13-16

May the LORD bless his land with the
precious dew from heaven above and
with the deep waters that lie below;
with the best the sun brings forth and
the finest the moon can yield;
with the choicest gifts of the
ancient mountains and the
fruitfulness of the everlasting hills;
with the best gifts of the earth
and its fullness and the favor of him
who dwelt in the burning bush.

LIFTING YOUR SPIRIT

Feel the Music

I mean come on, who doesn't love Live music? Music rejuvenates the mind, body and soul and can take your heart to places it has never been to. Music allows you to be you.

Feel the Positivity that flows through it, as it always makes you feel good. So, jump in the car and go out in search of some live music. I'm looking forward to seeing you somewhere, feeling the vibes of some good sounds.

Positive Thoughts, Positive Vibes!

People-Watching

I am all about people-watching. I love sitting back and watching the body language, the way people laugh, the way people look at each other… You can really collect some positive energy from watching people.

To be honest it just feels good to be able to be in the midst of people, to have those experiences. So why not soak it in? Why not take a sit back, grab a beverage and do a little people-watching?

Positive Thoughts, Positive Vibes!

KEEP MOVING

You know that "No parking on the dance floor" by Midnight Star, is one of my favorite songs. It just moves through your body in a way and that booty start to shake.

Just like in life, you need to keep those juices flowing, energize your mind, body, and soul and get to groovin. The hook will have you shaking yourself in the right direction, putting you around the right people and allowing you to get your mojo back. Like the song says, "it's so easy to rock baby" you are the DJ in control of the right mix that will keep you moving on the dance floor.

I Feel Good

James Brown said it best "I feel good." You know what? I feel so good I started dancing and singing in the living room. Don't go laughing at me, I do that often LOL. That's how good I felt.

I'm not sure of the source but it really doesn't matter sometimes. Soak up the good and let those good vibes flow. Dance, sing and laugh your way into allowing your spirit to get the juice it needs. Get those feet moving and feel-good baby.

Positive Thoughts, Positive Vibes!

START LIVIN'

Have you spent most of your life giving it away? Hoping instead of living? Your best life is in the present, present of being presence.

Find joy in the little things, embrace those dreams and revelations that allow you to live in the now. Your living starts today. The past is behind you, and none of us have the power to predict the future.

Living your best life starts from within. Opening your heart for peace, a peace that only you can find. Go get your peace and start livin' my friend, no more existing!

Positive Thoughts, Positive Vibes!

IT'S ALL ABOUT BALANCE!

Your ability to grow comes from surrounding yourself with good people. Like-minded means people who think alike or have the same view point. We also need folks who think differently to challenge the norm.

It's all about balance! Opposites do attract but they find common ground in acceptance. Understanding one another is key to creating peaceful environments. Most people want the best for themselves and by releasing positive energy, you will attract positive people.

MOVING IN THE RIGHT DIRECTION

We all go through hard times but if we're prayerful and patience enough we will get through it. Step away or stepping aside can allow enough time to see a little light. I know the road is not so smooth right now but like the pastor said "you have a friend in the Lord."

Take a moment and allow him to order your steps. He can help you see the situation from a different perspective. Trouble don't last always, keep stirring things up, moving forward. The pot holes, detours and road blocks all have to be fixed at some point.

Glad to see you moving in the right direction.

GET BACK YOUR GROOVE

Yes, the feeling is REAL! Your heart feels like it has been torn into pieces, how do you reclaim it? You loved so hard that you lost yourself in the process. You forgot what you like, loved and the person that shined on the inside. Everyone loved your smile and they wonder where did it go? You got this!

The extraordinary person is still hanging out inside of you. Just trapped, but today you got those juices flowing. The negative energy that is consuming you is making its way out. It looks like you even have a new step, singing an old tune that makes your heart sing.

Getting back into your groove feels real, so take back what is yours and allow those positive feelings to guide you.

THE BEST KIND OF MEDICINE

I love seeing people happy. Laughing, singing and even dancing. You know when you're in the grocery store and you walk down that aisle and they're playing your favorite song and there you go. You're picking up your favorite cereal box while singing that tune. It's almost like no one is watching. You're living in the moment, enjoying the little things without thinking.

That's what being happy is all about. Laugh, sing and dance whenever possible, living in the moment is the best kind of medicine.

Changing Your Attitude

Don't Look Back

I think the group, Boston, said it best, "don't look back". Today is a new day. The past is in the past, and a new day is breakin'. Yes, you feel great, refreshed, energized and on a new path. It's all about balance, step over those potholes, swerve around that road block and keep moving forward.

You haven't felt this good in a long time so embrace the new you. Nothing is gonna hold you down now because the present feels good and it's propelling you into the future. You're breathing new air so don't look back.

CREATE THE CHANGE

Here I go again, I am struggling to get to the gym. I know how important it is to eat right and exercise but I am really struggling. How do I get motivated? Should I just buy a size up in those jeans LOL.

It's all about baby steps my friend. Rome wasn't built in a day…. Don't move too fast or too slow. It's done at your own pace and maybe with a little assistance. Grab a friend, and also think outside the box. Take a walk, hike or even a few sit-ups while watching your favorite show. You don't have to do it all at once. This is a marathon baby! With the right mindset and a little support, you will start to create the change you want to see.

Positive Thoughts, Positive Vibes!

FIND THAT SMILE

Ain't it funny how the way you feel shows on your face. Back with the oldies my favorite group of all time Earth, Wind and Fire. You know some us out there cannot hide how we feel. It's written all over your face. The energy you exude can tell me it's not a good day. You're having a hard time seeing all the good things around you because that one thing has you stuck. But that's not enough to get you down, you've been there before my friend. I'm here to find that smile of yours so you can wear it well as you get through this one. It's time to sing a new song, move those two left feet and understand you got this. You don't want to be here living in the midst of sadness, not when there in joy right around the corner. Time is precious so push aside the negative and allow the positive to change what's on your face.

EMBRACE THE CHANGE

It looks like you're ready to love again. You've made yourself a priority, surrounded by good people and things are aligning in the right direction. Change can create the much-needed shift in how you look at things, giving you the right mindset ready for love. Not gonna repeat the same old patterns that didn't work in the past because the new you won't allow it.

That's right letting go of the past, living in the present and watch the positive vibes flow. Accept the good, embrace the change and keep loving yourself. Being ready to love hasn't every felt this good!

EMBRACING THE NEW YOU

Look how beautiful you are. Today is the day you decided to accept the person that you see in the mirror. Your smile, eyes, hair it all belongs to you. Embrace the person that God made. You look pretty darn good to me. Your beauty lies within; your soul shines because you appreciate the progress that's been made.

POSITIVE THOUGHTS, POSITIVE VIBES!

THE PEACE WITHIN

Stop giving away your peace. You all know it's very difficult to find peace or what might be considered your peace. Once you do, you must own it, protect and create those boundaries.

Yes, we all need help, support and to give, but protecting your peace through the process is essential. Some might not understand it but your ability to give back comes from the peace you have within.

POSITIVE THOUGHTS, POSITIVE VIBES!

IN THE MIRROR

Take a look in the mirror, don't you look fabulous? Of course, you do. You are an amazing, loving, caring and giving person.

It's so important to take moment and look in the mirror and say I'm a beautiful, awesome person. I'm strong, kind, free spirited, and accepting. Yes, accepting of who I am now, and the continued growth which is fine-tuning this amazing person that I see in the mirror.

POSITIVE THOUGHTS, POSITIVE VIBES!

SEE THE SIGNS

I miss my daddy…. when we lose a loved one, they will always be missed. But like they say, he is always with me. I know why, 'cause there goes the feather. That feather my dad kept in his truck and every once in a while, that feather will pop up. I can be leaving the grocery store, mowing the lawn or sitting in my backyard. At the right moment and time, that feather will pop up. That loved one will send you a sign, letting you know it's ok. It's ok to move on and keep living. Pay attention to the little signs they leave; the beauty of their spirit will always be with you.

POSITIVE THOUGHTS, POSITIVE VIBES!

AN AWESOME DAY

Man, I am on a roll today. Everything is going just fine. Everything is working out. I have had some great conversations with some amazing people. All of my things are getting done. Today is what I'm calling an amazing day.

Sometimes we need to take some time and recognize those awesome days when they happen. Yeah, I know, not every day is going to feel like today, but today I recognize it as being an awesome day. We can take those positive juices to help propel us through those tough times. So, you know what my friends? I am gonna soak up this awesome day and spread a little sunshine with it.

YOU DAY

Today was the best day, do you know why? Because I took some time to focus on me. I called off of work, went back home and jumped right into bed, LOL.

Minimize the noise of the world and dive in for some peace. A little "me time" is so important to keep yourself balanced for the things ahead. I know the list is long, and so many things to do but don't forget the "me time." Once you have rested in bed for a little, head over to that happy place, grab some dinner or drink or just spend some time doing nothing. Today was the best day because I took a little time out for me.

LOVE AND UNITY!

In this crazy world we live in, sometimes we forget that love conquers hate and unity eliminates division. We must be open to building bridges, instead of perpetuating hate, anger and ignorance.

Through love comes understanding and the ability to see past ourselves. We cannot let our egos cloud a pathway of being open-minded.

You control what you feel for others. Can you see their beauty or just their faults? Can you see beyond what might hurt and see what can heal?

Start with positivity and see what you get!

POSITIVE THOUGHTS, POSITIVE VIBES!

Pop up – Dive in

In the movie Lion Guard Bunga sang "Zuka Zama". It's a funny little song with lots of meaning. In Swahili it means, "Pop up, dive in."

Today may be your day to pop up and dive in. Dive in and let your heart sing and your soul feel. Open up and breathe new air and new life in the old life you have been living. Love the new life that's in right in front of you. Sing that song, dance that dance. Zuka Zuma might just be the song you need to wake up and dive in.

Positive Thoughts, Positive Vibes!

TAKE THE LEAP

I'm sitting here and you know I have it figured out. Go left, go right, go any which way. Life can have you twisting and turning in all different directions. You second guess your moves, ask for suggestions and it's just not feeling right.

Take the leap! What do you have to lose? Ok it might not work out the way you planned it but it might work out for the best. Yes, I wrote that book, I cleaned up my resume, I changed careers. Really guys, who has it all figured out? Today… just go with it and start living. I bet something is gonna work out and I'm thinking the change will be good.

LEANING ON OTHERS

CLAIM TODAY

The Lord said it, 'and bless it be to rock and let the God of my salvation be exalted'. Today is the day that you claim it. You claim the victory, happiness, and your peace. Look upon the Lord because the victory is yours. That new job, new book you're going to write and that new relationship right around the corner. Enjoy the positive energy flowing because you gave him the praise first "when the praises go up, the blessing come down."

POSITIVE THOUGHTS, POSITIVE VIBES!

GIVE ME A HUG

Hug me baby, hug me tight… it feels so good to be able to offer up and to receive a hug. We've been through some tough times, my friends, but it feels great to be able to offer up a hug, a smile, a kind word. I mean so good to be able to get close to one another again. From the zoom calls, to video chats, now we have the opportunity to offer up a hug, so come on over here and please give me a hug!

POSITIVE THOUGHTS, POSITIVE VIBES!

THE GAZE

It was just a simple gaze that sparked the connection. Yes, you saw it. Our eyes met for a split second. My attention was focused on you when you noticed my gaze. They say “the Gaze” is a powerful element of social interaction. What was the emotional effect? What role did the gaze play in our social connection? It was an opportunity to allow your inner spirit to be vulnerable to what ‘could be’.

Don’t look away. No need to be nervous. Look into my eyes and witness the things I see, feel and want. A simple gaze in the right direction could be exactly what the doctor ordered. Enjoy the Positive Vibes flowing through you and the power of the gaze someone has to offer. Vanish any negative energies.

Truly Loving

Sometimes we love so hard that we don't allow enough room - "Room" for the love to grow and manifest into whatever form it will be. Patrice Rushen said it best, "maybe we need just a little room".

One of the major components of truly loving someone is friendship. Allowing time for the friendship to grow will provide the understanding needed for the love to blossom. Let your heart feel with eyes open and your soul ready. That's right, no need to look back at what could have been, allow the time for the connection to flourish. In time it will show itself and enjoy the beauty in whatever form that might be.

THE POWER OF A HUG!

There's nothing like a good hug from someone with positive energy. It can go through you and make everything ok. I know some of you don't like to be touched. Touch shows that someone cares, so you need to open up and allow that in.

A hug from the right person can make a world of difference. It's an unspoken gesture that offers comfort and makes the soul feel good. You must remember it's very important to take care of your soul. If your inside feels good then your outside will shine. And yes, we all need to see that light of yours shining bright.

POSITIVE THOUGHTS, POSITIVE VIBES!

LET YOUR LIGHT SHINE

Wake up and decide to be you. That's right, I'm going to offer the world the real deal. I'm not going to sit and wonder if people will like it or not.

Is what I have to offer worthy enough? I need to make everyone happy with what they see on the outside. Your mindset may be in the wrong place. It's on the outside and you already forgot about the inside. That's where the real you is! Let that light shine baby and attract the ones who deserve it. If it works for them that's cool, if not, keep on keeping on!

POWER OF LOVE

We meet people for a reason. They can become a blessing or a lesson on our journey. Taking the time to understand one another is a form of LOVE. Our differences become less obvious and the unknown more common.

There is an old saying, "Love thy neighbor," and we are all neighbors looking for the same thing in life. There is an opportunity to show love and be loved.

Share a little love today. Offer a smile, a kind word or a helping hand. Fill your soul with positive energy and you will experience the power of LOVE.

POSITIVE THOUGHTS, POSITIVE VIBES!

Freely Connecting

I wander at times. The Spirit leads me to random places where I get to make meaningful connections with strangers. Sometimes these connections are for a moment, sometimes they are for a lifetime.

We know that every single connection has meaning and purpose. Allow people to come in and out of your lives, freely, for these connections offer growth, and through that growth you gain wisdom.

When Strangers Become Friends

You call that person your friend who was once a stranger. You connected for a reason. How we view, interrupt or accept the connection is up to us. We need to allow ourselves to be vulnerable and open to the unlimited possibilities of the connection.

We were all strangers at one point and allowed ourselves to feel, like, love and acquire a friendship with someone. Being open to the connection can take your mind, body and soul to new heights.

TRUE LOVE

I just love the song by champagne "how about us". Some people are made for each other. Some people can love one another for life. How about us? I love hearing the stories of couples who have been together 40 and 50 years.

I asked a question how do you do it? How do you stay together for so long? Most say living a simple life, communication, compromise and be true to yourself and your partner.

It's a beautiful thing to behold true love between two people, the love that can last through all kinds of weather.

PILLOW TALK

Pillow talk. What is pillow talk? They say it's an opportunity where you can sit down with someone and just completely open up. Having that safe space where you can talk about anything and everything.

We all wish and hope for that someone that we can talk with. To lay our heads on a pillow, relax and have the opportunity to completely be ourselves. That's what it's all about, the opportunity to completely be yourself, and be in that safe space, to let someone else know what you're thinking, feeling or desire.

SOMETHING ABOUT YOU

I love the song by Lakeside, "There's something about that woman." You know the one, that special someone that you think about often. You're pretty fond of her, the way she talks, walks and makes you feel. Allowing yourself to be open, free and absorbing the positive vibes she has to offer. It's that crazy feeling deep down inside the pit of your stomach. Something about that woman moves you, inspires you, provides the completeness within you. Something about that woman touches your soul, only you can feel. If you every had a real love, then you know there's something about that woman that makes your heart sing. Beholding the beauty of allowing yourself to feel, gives the opportunity to appreciate the true love.

GIVE YOUR SOUL!

One of the greatest gifts someone can give is their soul. It means they completely trust you, and feel comfortable with who you are and where you are.

The ability to be vulnerable from within, and allowing your feelings to be shared can be terrifying. It means sharing your deepest thoughts, wants, desires. The effects of life experiences have shaped you. You are a different person today than you were yesterday.

Hopefully you will be blessed with that opportunity to be freed, in order to be free.

A Real Connection

A simple encounter can lead to friendship for life. You had no idea that the person you just met would have your back for life. Why do we connect with some and not others? What makes a connection special or above the rest?

We see similarities in people that draw us in. It could be a spiritual, work, or other connection. There are many different reasons why we connect. The spirit of that person could be easy like Sunday morning. If the connection is real, then just looking within will provide the answer. We met for a reason and our connection has purpose. Enjoy the simplicity of it.

What You Desire

KEEP SMILING

I know you see the smile on my face. My two boys bring me so much joy. When God blesses you with such perfection, all you can do is smile. We laugh, we cry, we talk and we walk. We keep our eyes on the future with nothing but positive thoughts flowing. I give them my best and they do the same. I'm just gonna keep on smiling, because smiling makes me feel good and it shows. I'm living my best life because of my boys.

POSITIVE THOUGHTS, POSITIVE VIBES!

I Got Your Back

I thought we were friends? You told me I was your best friend, the one you could turn to in your time of need. But it feels like the friendship has fizzled. You have turned cold and distant. I continue to reach out and offer comfort but you turn me away.

What happened to understanding that true friendship means opening up when things get tough? Now is not the time to push me away, instead, bring me in close. I'm here for you. Know that my friendship is true.

I got your back!

SOME AMAZING CONVERSATION

I left saying, "WOW! That was awesome, amazing just the best." My spirit felt so good and I'm leaving with so much positive juice flowing though me…

You're probably wondering, where was that version of me? I just had some amazing conversation, that's it. Great conversation with someone who's spirit has the same energy. You know that feeling when you don't want the conversation to end? Yup, that's what it was, some amazing conversation. Let's keep those juices flowing.

POSITIVE THOUGHTS, POSITIVE VIBES!

WHAT ARE YOU WAITING FOR?

I'm living my best life now. You know why, because I'm being me. Giving the world the best I have to offer, and not looking back.

You can feel and see my light shine brightly. Allow the energy I'm giving off you, positively inspire you to do the same. Today is the day you start living your best life. It's all right there for the taking. What are you waiting for?

POSITIVE THOUGHTS, POSITIVE VIBES!

Don't Hide It

Don't be afraid to show off your beauty. I see you feeling good about the way you look today. Show it off, walk out of the house with that fresh new glow. That smile of yours has the ability to change someone's day, so wear it.

Why are you hiding? What is keeping you from giving the world your best? Are you listening to others? The ones who are not lifting you up? The ones who are not filling your cup? No more my friend, look for the ones who support your glow, your shine because it's unique. It's yours so own, share it, and believe it.

WHAT YOU OFFER

I woke up this morning and realized that God has a greater plan for me. I believe in me. I honor who I am and I continue my growth to see all of the gifts that he has bestowed upon me. These gifts I continue to share with the world. I embrace the power that they behold. Forever thankful, forever appreciative of all of the things that I have around me, which is giving me the opportunity to give. What are my gifts? What do I have to offer to the world? Start with just being you! Think about the things you are passionate about and run with that. You will have the ability to give, to grow and to impact so many people… it will be the best feeling ever.

LIFE RIGHT NOW

You know what? I'm not sure I know what I want. I mean, what is life all about? What is the life I want to live? Maybe it's the life I'm living.

Did I miss it? Life might be pretty good right now? I like my job, my kiddos are great, I'm breathing, clothes on my back, etc. You know what? I think I like "this life right now." It's pretty darn good once you take a step back and appreciate all the wonderful things you have.

POSITIVE THOUGHTS, POSITIVE VIBES!

It Is Happening

Life is happening. If you let life happen without you, you won't be the only one who suffers. You're probably like what the heck does he mean? Let me explain.

When there are so many good things going on, I mean one after the next, and you miss them, you miss out.

You're about to explode and it's hard to stay present. It's got you all over the place even looking into the future for what is next. It's the perfect time to sit back and soak it in.

Yes, it's happening and without a negative vibe in the air.

PUSHING THROUGH

Life is not perfect, we've all seen our share of ups and downs. Life's challenges and experiences have shaped us into what we are today. I've shared many of mine through my writings in Positive Vibes 1 and 2. I'm forever grateful for the many conversations I've had with you all. The stories you have shared, inspire me to write about our day to day being.

Yes, we strive every day to be the best we can be. Some days are harder than others, but we push through. That's what it's all about, pushing through and moving forward. This Positive Vibes movement hopes to sprinkle in a little positivity along your journey. Together we each can keep encouraging and motivating the world!

THE IMPORTANCE OF CONNECTION

Our ability to connect is so important in our day-to-day living. That connection allows us to conduct business and establish friendships.

Through growth, we understand ourselves better which allows us to continue to build positive connections; dissolving the ones that tear us down.

The best connections let you be you, which will attract the best people to travel on your journey with you.

POSITIVE THOUGHTS, POSITIVE VIBES!

YOUR PRIORITIES

What are priorities? Things that are urgent can cloud our priorities. Nothing shapes us more than focusing on the need and not the want.

A person on their death bed sees the world differently. Understanding that every moment is precious, the foggy glasses become very clear. The priorities become simple and the journey less rocky.

Take a step back and allow the power of the now to help you focus on what is important.

POSITIVE THOUGHTS, POSITIVE VIBES.

WORKING IT YOUR WAY

Everybody knows I love some old R&B Earth Wind & Fire, Spinners, Commodores, all of that good stuff. I hear the Spinners "I'm working my way back to you babe." Well, I'm not sure about that one Lol. Sometimes it might be worth moving forward, right? Working your way back might not help you turn into the person you need to be today. I hear ya, that burning love inside might not be at the right temperature or is for the right person.

Take some time to work on you, fine tune the things and create the space needed for your present self. Something is burning inside of you and that is change, the change that will put you in some really good spaces. I see you putting a new spin on an old song, "working it your way."

PROTECT THE PEACE

As I'm creeping up to the big 50, many people ask me what are you looking for? And my answer is always; peace. I'm looking to be in the midst of peaceful situations and as many peaceful people as I can be around.

It's not always easy to find peace in a world filled with so much noise. So, it's very important that we balance our lives and surround ourselves with peaceful oriented people.

You know, people who are in search of peace as well. The ones who are in continued growth mode, fine tuning themselves from within and letting go of the negative.

Protecting your peace is priceless!

Paying Attention

KEEP IT REAL

To me, "Love me today, leave me tomorrow," sounds like a sad old song. Not today! Figure out if your love and friendship is true.

You can be sure; I will not be the same person you left. My heart is big and it's here for you, but the back and forth is not working anymore. Enough is enough. My mind, body and soul deserve to have positive energies for someone or something that is true. So today I'm taking care of me and making sure I'm in the right space. Keep it real or keep it moving.

POSITIVE THOUGHTS, POSITIVE VIBES!

SHARE YOUR GIFTS

I see you flying, I mean, soaring along in life. They say some birds are not meant to be caged. Your feathers are just too bright and there is a little bit of an ambitious, spontaneous side about you. Not everyone gets you or understands the way you walk and talk. It's on a whole different vibration; you groove and move different from the rest. It's beautiful when you get it. I mean, get who you are and what your purpose in life is. You share your gifts and allow the world to experience your spirit just the way God gave it to you. Surround yourself with the people who see it too, and your feathers will continue to grow, and the beauty of your spirit shall shine.

OUR PURPOSE IN LIFE

It is a good question and sometimes, we are not sure what the answer is. YOU hold the answer to what your purpose in life is. Your vision becomes clear when you tap in and look within. Most people work all their lives and dislike what they do.

Passion is the driving force to your dreams and the ability to be happy. Seek what you love and what you are passionate about.

Try to find what makes you feel alive and turn your passion into reality. Sing a song and allow the music from within to guide you.

Positive Thoughts, Positive Vibes!

TEACHABLE MOMENTS

You know that special someone, the one that ignites something in us that no one else has ever done? He or she touched your soul in a way that no one else ever had. When you go to sleep at night, you think of them. When you wake up in the morning, it's the same feeling.

There is always a reason why someone comes into our lives at a certain time. They're giving you the ability to feel deep down inside your soul. These types of relationships help us with growth. They give us the ability to feel, give and have a glimpse of what love feels like. Those types of relationships provide the teachable moments, which will help us with future connections.

WHAT WILL YOUR ATTITUDE BE TODAY?

You have the power to choose what your attitude is. You can alter your life by changing your attitude. Your outlook and perception can not only impact you but also the people you connect with.

Is your attitude worth catching? If not, how can you tap in and make sure what you give is what you want to receive.

Maintaining a positive attitude is not always easy, but it can be done.

Positive Thoughts, Positive Vibes!

MAKING STRIDES

Today is the day you make the first step. God promised if you make the first step, He will make the second. You are making strides to add a little more positivity in your life. Join the positive vibes movement and continue to do the things you need to do to live the life you want.

Create that vibe tribe of genuine people and allow them to support and inspire you moving forward. Step one today, will lead to many more steps moving forward. Continue making strides and allow your passion for living your best life to shine.

POSITIVE THOUGHTS, POSITIVE VIBES!

WHAT IS YOUR PASSION?

Your passion will take you to places you have never been before. When you allow it to take over, nothing and no one can hold you back.

To some, it may be work or a chore but to you, it is you. The things you are passionate about order your steps in the direction of happiness. What you feel inside is like nothing else. To be honest, it's sometimes hard to even put it into words.

Passion is a beautiful thing that lives in all of us, it's time to let your passion shine!

POSITIVE THOUGHTS, POSITIVE VIBES.

BE KIND

Today is your day to be kind. A single act of kindness can have a positive rippling effect.

Share of yourself and the next person may share with someone else. People talk about karma. What we do now can come back to affect us later.

It's not about being self-absorbed but rather, giving of yourself which will allow a peaceful spirit to take over. Being kind frees your spirit and unlocks the chains and negativity.

POSITIVE THOUGHTS, POSITIVE VIBES.

I HEAR YA!

You had your life all planned out and it's not looking anything like you imagined. Married, kids, successful job, big house, fancy car, etc.... The issue is, you were moving too fast.

Remember that living in the now is always the best because we cannot predict the future. When we move too fast we forget to see all of the awesome things around us now.

You have the power to control the present which might help with the future. Live, love and enjoy what you have now and allow that positive energy to lead you into the future.

POSITIVE THOUGHTS, POSITIVE VIBES.

THE UNKNOWN

How important are the people you surround yourself with? The right person can see something in you that you don't see in yourself. I mean, put you on a path that you never expected. A friend of mine said " I had a feeling about you" that feeling was something special. An unknown road traveled with unlimited possibilities. Stepping into the unknown can be scary but with the right people around you, the support will propel you forward. It's time to step out on faith and see what God has in store for you. Recognizing your gifts, honing them, fine tuning them, and once done, sharing them. Sharing those gifts might just give someone else the spark to travel down that unknown pathway.

TRUE FRIENDS

There is truth in true friendship.

We hear people talk about it all the time. You know what, so-and-so is my true friend. But what accounts for true friendship? What makes a person a true friend? It's the person that highlights the positives and minimizes the negative. Offers a helping hand but doesn't enable you. The one who reaches out to you because being in your presence just makes them feel better. The one that will hold you accountable when needed. It's that feel-good person that needs nothing more than to soak up your good vibes. There is truth in friendship with the ones that make your soul shine.

Your Purpose

UNSPOKEN CONNECTION

Thank you for being such an amazing friend. That person I can depend on. Even during the tough times, having that special someone is so important. It's also wonderful when they highlight those good times in your life.

True friendship is all about understanding and respect, allowing each other the space and time to understand one another. Sharing a few words or just being silent, "balance" is the key which helps you understand the differences as well. You get it, it's an unspoken connection.

POSITIVE THOUGHTS, POSITIVE VIBES!

Feeling Blessed

I think Fred Hammond said it best "You are the living word." Yes, one of the greatest gifts my mother gave me was introducing me to the living God. No matter the situation, I know I have a friend in Jesus.

I have found myself on many occasions calling his name. He was sent down from glory to be light for us in our time of need, and to rejoice during the happy times. Feeling blessed to call him my friend. His grace allows me to give of myself and shine my light in hopes of inspiring others.

Positive thoughts, positive vibes.

Rejoice Always

1 Thessalonians 5:16-18

Rejoice always, pray continually,
give thanks in all circumstances;
for this is God's will for you
in Christ Jesus.

FREE YOURSELF

Be free, feel free.

It's no fun waking up every morning thinking about fifty million problems to solve. Or carrying around burdens and guilt about something you said or did.

You are the only one who can free yourself from it all. Allow at least a few moments a day to feel free.

Some problems you will have to let go of and understand that we don't always say or do the right things. You give the world YOU; the best you have to offer. That has to be good enough!

POSITIVE THOUGHTS, POSITIVE VIBES!

GIVING BACK

Many of you know the story by now. My father passed away in 2015 from a massive heart attack. Some might say, as a form of therapy, I started writing and posting Positive messages on social media. My friend and publisher, Kathleen J. Shields said you need to write a book. So ever since I've been writing these short daily affirmations.

My two books are written for the non-reader. You can read a message every day or breeze through the book in one evening. We all have something to share. Giving back is so important to me. Our foundation has been impacting families since 2002. Feel free to share this message along with any of the daily affirmations I post. Together we will sprinkle a little more Positive Vibes into the world.

THE ROAD TRAVELED

It's not about the destination, but the road traveled. It's not about where you are going but how you get there. That includes all of the pit stops and fill-ups along the way. These things help shape and prepare you for what is waiting.

Things always have a way of working themselves out. The pot holes, road closures and detours are a part of the journey. Continue to move forward and stay focused. You will be surprised where the road leads you.

POSITIVE THOUGHTS, POSITIVE VIBES.

CHOOSE THE LIFE YOU LIVE

We all have control of the type of life we want to live. Most of us would love to live a happy life filled with positivity. Of course, there will be some bumps in the road, but our choices decide that.

Also, things that you have no control of will try to consume you. Allow how you would like to live to lead the way.

Take a few minutes every morning to balance yourself with positive thoughts that will keep you on the right path. Remember you have the power to live the best life you want.

Positive Thoughts, Positive Vibes!

YOUR TIME IS NOW!

There is a reason that you are still here. What does being still here really mean?

Your thoughts, beliefs, dreams and vision of the life you want are still here. They are still in the present waiting for you to start living.

Are you stuck? Stuck in the "what if" zone?

Get up and start living. Put that plan in place and move forward. Leave those troubles behind and put your positive hat on.

Your time is now!

POSITIVE THOUGHTS, POSITIVE VIBES.

FILL YOUR TANK

Are you running low on fumes or on empty? Do the daily tasks of the week have you feeling spent?

What will you do to rejuvenate your mind, body and soul? At the end of the day, you can only do what you can do.

Don't continue to run low on fumes and burn out. Stop and listen to your body and get those juices flowing again.

The world needs the best YOU have to offer!

POSITIVE THOUGHTS, POSITIVE VIBES!

To the Beach

Why do we feel so connected to the beach? Being around water gives our brains a chance to rest and have a positive effect on our soul. The sun soaking on your skin releases those feel-good chemicals throughout your body.

My good friend Jackie Bieber says, “There's just something about the waves, the size of the ocean and how small we are. Even the salty air and the breeze, just completely restores and refreshes my soul"

Warm sand, gentle waves and soothing ambiance there is simply no better place to let go of daily stress than heading to the beach.

SOUND OF WATER

TLC said it best, "Don't go chasing waterfalls." What's already downstream is past you. Sometimes in life, we need to slow down and allow things to unfold.

Following the wrong things or wrong people can lead you down a path of uncertainty. Your heart will never fail you and living your best life is what you need to strive for. Most people just exist, and don't take the opportunity to live.

Take a moment to breathe and listen to the sounds around you. The rain can be soothing, just like a trickling stream or the ocean. The waves can provide a simple sounding board that will keep you on the right path.

Reference: *Line sung by* TLC *in the song* "Waterfalls" *Album* "CrazySexyCool"*1994*

GET MOVING

BE A HELPER

I woke up this morning and I am grateful for my amazing friends who support and encourage me every day.

Mr. Rogers said it best "look for the helpers today." I choose to be a helper and offer a helping hand to someone in need. Working together we can achieve some amazing things and make the world a better place.

Positive Thoughts, Positive Vibes!

Focus on the Good

Look in the mirror and appreciate the beautiful person that you see. You are amazing just the way you are. Always be confident in yourself and trust in your abilities. Believe that you can achieve anything that you set your mind to.

When you focus on the good and you allow the positive vibes to come in, you are capable of doing great things.

Keep smiling and keep shining.

Positive Thoughts, Positive Vibes!

Embrace God's Path

Good morning, everyone!

Sometimes life takes us in an unexpected yet welcomed path.

Blessings come when you least expect it.

Embrace Gods path.

It was designed for you and you only!

Positive Thoughts, Positive Vibes!

THE RIGHT PERSON

Sometimes we want to love, or be loved, but understanding and accepting it can be difficult. It could take that special someone to love you in a way that allows your heart to open up.

Jon B. said it best "you gave me someone to love." Yes, the right person, loving the true you, in turn gives you the opportunity to take a chance on love. And that is beautiful!

POSITIVE THOUGHTS, POSITIVE VIBES!

THE TOUCH

It was once desired that he touched her soul in a way only she would know. The exchange of energy between two people provides the opportunity for one's soul to be touched. Not only physical touch but through emotions, provides that one of kind connection that you have with no one else.

It's special! Something that words cannot describe, it's an unspoken profound effect that the two people have for one another. They show up at a significant time in your life and offer a sense of peace like no other. The love is so strong that you adore everything about them. It's all about accepting their flaws, imperfections and everything about them.

APPROACH ADVERSITY

There is an old saying that "time heals all wounds". Things have been pretty tough for you, the journey traveled has had some bumps in the road. When you hit rock bottom there is only one way that's up. Your ability today to remove toxic energies, look at salutations from different perspectives and believe in YOU!

Sometimes you need to use "time" to give the ability to get through those tough times. You are using your time more wisely and this is the main factor in seeing the change you want to see. In our lifetime we will go through adversity but how we approach it is key. Give yourself time to look within and find what you need, moving forward with more positive vibes flowing.

MAGIC OF KINDNESS

It doesn't take much to be kind, and the positive, rippling effect of change can benefit one's life. Acts of kindness can make the world a happier place for everyone. They can boost feelings of confidence, being in control, happiness and optimism. They may also encourage others to repeat the good deeds they've experienced themselves – contributing to a more positive community.

Just a thought… sprinkling in those positive vibes is like adding something to a delicious pot of soup. All of the ingredients come together to make something special. Today is your day to add something to your pot and watch, smell and taste the magic of kindness.

GRACE

Because of grace, I stand here today! What is grace? Grace gets me through my struggles. Grace allows me to be me. You accepted this imperfect person and say it's ok. It's ok to be you, because God has got your back.

Grace allows us to give the world the best we have to offer and fine tune those things we need to. God loves us for who we are and he wants you to stand tall and love who you are today. Today is your day to love you!

Positive Thoughts, Positive Vibes!

ACTS OF KINDNESS

Every year there is a National Acts of Kindness Day. We did an amazing social media push encouraging everyone to discuss different ways to be kinder to each other. Remember acts of the kindness is a part of our everyday living.

Show love, share a hug, send a card, check in on a neighbor. Take a moment to think of others, pay it forward and encourage someone else to do the same. Allow your light to shine to positively impact others, spread that sunshine and help move those clouds out of the way. Be true in the love you share and allow the rippling effect to create the change you want to see.

EMBRACE THE POWER

I can see us sitting there, holding hands, sipping on a drink, getting lost in the flames without the need to say a word. It's a beautiful unusual mild winter night, with a slight breeze in the air.

There is something about being outside in nature with the warmth of the fire. The sense of peace consumes us bringing about stillness. Allow for the moments to take hold of you and embrace the power they hold.

POSITIVE THOUGHTS, POSITIVE VIBES.

TAKE A CHANCE

How beautiful is it when someone truly loves you? I mean, truly loves the person from within. Not a fantasy, dream or someone from your favorite romance novel. The feeling when someone is in "Awe" of you! Revered, admired, adored, appreciated, cherished, the list goes on. Your ability to feel safe in their presence, completely comfortable in being who you are and what you offer. No judgement, a safe space of vulnerability that will allow your love to grow.

POSITIVE THOUGHTS, POSITIVE VIBES!

MAKE ROOM FOR GOOD

I was driving down the street and Jonathan McReynolds said, "I will make room for you." Today is the day when you can move it over. You have to allow space for the good to come in. Negativity will take over and not allow your mind, body and soul to be still. In order to see and feel your blessings, you need some still time. Push aside as much as you can and let the good that is there shine through. Make the first step and God will help with the next one.

POSITIVE THOUGHTS, POSITIVE VIBES!

THANK YOU

It's so important to take the time out to say thank you. You are never too busy to say thank you. Always take the time out to tell someone you appreciate them for who they are, and everything that they've done for you.

Thank you might not seem like much, but just the ability to say thank you to someone, just to show that you appreciate everything that they do for you is so important. People want to feel appreciated. By saying thank you or offering a kind word, that's how you do it.

Thank you for just being you!

TODAY IS YOUR DAY

It is often said, "Tomorrow is not promised and today is short." It is easier said than done to focus on today and not think about tomorrow.

We spend most of our time planning for the future and not enjoying the blessings we have today. In the blink of an eye, your world can turn upside down.

Today is the day. Love more, live more and pray more. Hold no regrets because what God has in store for tomorrow is not yours to control. He has given you today to see your blessings.

POSITIVE THOUGHTS, POSITIVE VIBES.

IT'S TIME!!!

It's time to jump! That's right, time to jump. What are you waiting for, the perfect moment, time or place? The stars may never align unless you jump. Yes, you might disappoint a few folks, be judged, or even be laughed at. But now is the best time. You will never know what lies ahead if you don't.

Something better is waiting on the other side. Go start that business, write that book, fall in love and even fly across the world. Today is your day to jump into the future with a whole new outlook.

Philippians 4:8

Finally, brothers and sisters,
whatever is true,
whatever is noble,
whatever is right,
whatever is pure,
whatever is lovely,
whatever is admirable
—if anything is excellent
or praiseworthy
—think about such things.

ABOUT THE AUTHOR

Preston Mitchum Jr. has dedicated his life to giving back and making a difference. Born in Bronx, New York his family moved to Langley Park, MD in 1981.

His family established the Mitchum Lawn and Landscaping business shortly after. This is where his father, Mitchum Sr. worked for over 30 years, creating beautiful lawns and establishing relationships throughout the community.

Preston Jr. is a graduate of Towson State University where he took his love for video and became an 18-year veteran news photographer for WMAR-TV in Baltimore, Maryland.

During this time, he founded The PMJ Foundation to create change in the Baltimore community. The foundation's vision is to impact families through programs and services that offer positive growth. The foundation has served thousands throughout Maryland.

With the passing of his father, Preston has taken over the family business and will continue to provide the quality service that his family established for many years.

~

A portion of the proceeds of this book
will support the programs that the
PMJ Foundation offers.

~

This book is dedicated to Preston's
two wonderful sons, Carter and Harrison.

~

Preston hopes that the positive message this book has to offer will impact thousands and create positive vibes that we all can feel.

THE PMJ FOUNDATION

PRESENTING POSSIBILITIES FOR BRIGHTER FUTURES

The PMJ Foundation's Career Awareness Project (CAP) after-school program brings the outside professional world into the classroom. Community volunteers present their careers to our participants which engage our at-risk youth to explore the infinite possibilities of college and career choices that are available.

~

To learn more about the PMJ Foundation please visit: **www.pmjfoundation.org**

ERIN GO BRAGH
Publishing

Erin Go Bragh Publishing publishes various genres of books for numerous authors. Their portfolio consists of a 1200-page Vietnamese to English Dictionary, Historical fiction, an award-winning children's educational series, multiple adult novels and memoires, tween adventure stories, as well as Christian Fiction. Their objective is to promote literacy and education through reading and writing.

REFERENCES

Made in the USA
Columbia, SC
01 November 2024

45487659R00083